W9-CBU-214

Fact Finders™

Biographies

Charles Drew
Pioneer in Medicine

by Laura Purdie Salas

Consultant:
Dr. Kenneth Goings, Professor and Chair
Department of African American and African Studies
The Ohio State University
Columbus, Ohio

Capstone press

Mankato, Minnesota

Fact Finders is published by Capstone Press,
151 Good Counsel Drive, P.O. Box 669, Mankato, Minnesota 56002.
www.capstonepress.com

Library of Congress Cataloging-in-Publication Data
Salas, Laura Purdie.
 Charles Drew : pioneer in medicine / by Laura Purdie Salas.
 p. cm. — (Fact finders. Biographies.)
 Includes bibliographical references and index.
 ISBN-13: 978-0-7368-5433-7 (hardcover)
 ISBN-10: 0-7368-5433-9 (hardcover)
 ISBN-13: 978-0-7368-6914-0 (softcover pbk.)
 ISBN-10: 0-7368-6914-X (softcover pbk.)
 1. Drew, Charles Richard, 1904–1950. 2. African American surgeons—Biography—
Juvenile literature. 3. Blood banks—United States—Juvenile literature. I. Title. II. Series.
RD27.35.D74S35 2006
617'.092—dc22   2005022578

Summary: An introduction to the life of Charles Drew, the African American doctor noted
 for his work with blood and blood plasma.

Editorial Credits
Megan Schoeneberger, editor; Juliette Peters, set designer; Linda Clavel and Scott Thoms,
 book designers; Kelly Garvin, photo researcher/photo editor

Photo Credits
Amherst College Archives and Special Collections, 9
Courtesy of Moorland-Spingarn Research Center, Howard University, 1, 7, 8, 15, 17, 19,
 21, 25, 27
Courtesy of the McGill University Archives, 4–5, 10–11, 12, 13
Getty Images Inc./Time Life Pictures, cover, 23
U.S. Postal Service, 26

1 2 3 4 5 6 11 10 09 08 07 06

Table of Contents

Chapter 1

The Race for Blood

Flames raced through Montreal General Hospital in Canada. Some of the patients were injured. They needed blood, and they needed it fast.

Charles Drew was a young doctor on duty that night in 1934. Drew struggled to find blood to give to the patients. There wasn't enough donated blood. He saved some lives, but other patients died.

For the next several years, Drew studied blood and blood **transfusions**. He wanted to find a better way to store blood. He didn't want any more patients to die because of blood shortages.

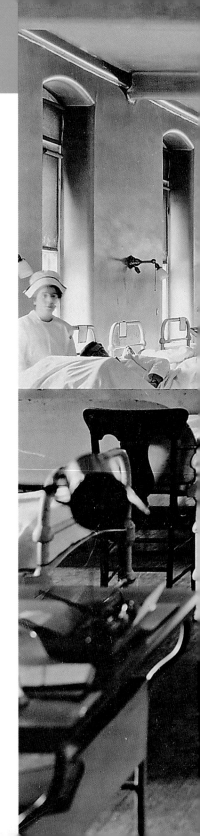

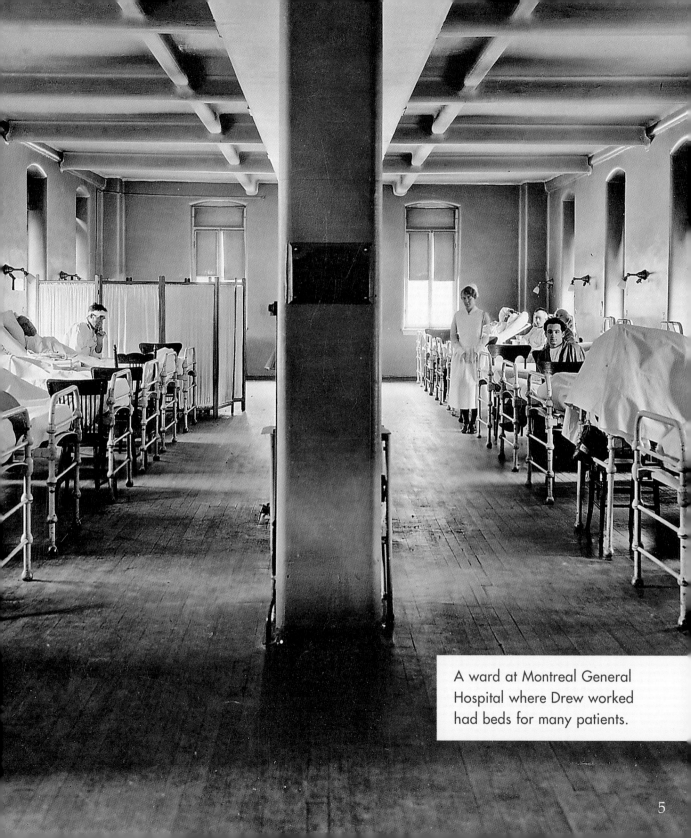

A ward at Montreal General Hospital where Drew worked had beds for many patients.

Chapter 2

Growing Up

Charles Richard Drew was born June 3, 1904, in Washington, D.C. His mother, Nora, was a schoolteacher. His father, Richard, was a carpet layer. Drew had four younger brothers and sisters.

School

Drew went to Stevens Elementary School. He loved sports. He won four swimming medals by the time he was 8 years old.

After elementary school, Drew went to Paul Laurence Dunbar High School. This school was segregated. Only black students attended.

Charles Drew (wearing necktie) was the oldest child in his family.

Drew played football for
Amherst College in 1923. ↓

Drew was very athletic.
He played football, basketball,
and baseball in high school.
He also ran on the track team.
Drew's classmates voted him
the school's best athlete.

College

Drew graduated from
high school in 1922. Later
that year, Drew started
classes at Amherst College
in Massachusetts.

Drew faced more **racism**
while in college. During his
junior year, the track team
went to Rhode Island. The
team ate at a restaurant that
served only white people.
The restaurant refused to
serve Drew.

▲ Drew (front, fourth from right) was the captain of the Amherst College track team.

Drew planned to be an engineer, but he changed his mind. He thought about his sister Elsie, who had died in 1920 after an illness. He became interested in healing. When Drew graduated from college in 1926, he wanted to go to medical school.

Chapter 3

Medical School

Drew could not afford medical school right away. He taught science at a college in Maryland for two years to save up money.

Medical School

Drew applied to Howard University Medical School in 1928. This school in Washington, D.C., was just for African Americans. The school turned Drew down. He had not taken enough English classes at Amherst College.

Harvard University was open to both white and African American students. Harvard was full, but it accepted him to attend the next year.

The Strathcona Medical Building is part of the McGill University campus.

Drew didn't want to wait another year. He applied to McGill University in Quebec, Canada. McGill accepted him right away.

Inspiring Professor

At McGill, Drew met a British teacher named John Beattie. Beattie researched blood transfusions.

Doctors faced two problems with transfusions. First, not every person can accept blood from every other person. The blood type of the donor has to be **compatible** with the blood type of the patient. If an injured person needed blood, doctors had to find a donor immediately. And they had to run tests to find out if the donor had the right blood type.

Second, blood storage was difficult. Hospitals could keep blood for only seven days before it went bad. Testing the blood types took time. While doctors frantically tried to find the right blood type, patients often died. Hospitals rarely had enough fresh blood for transfusions.

The problems of blood types and blood storage interested both Dr. Beattie and Drew. They began researching together.

DREW,
    CHARLES RICHARD
Born in Washington, D.C. Educated in public schools in D.C., graduating from High School in 1922. B.A. from Amherst College, Amherst, Mass., 1926. Instructor in Biology and coach 1926-'28. Entered McGill 1928. Member of track club 1928-'33, captain 1931. Student representative to athletic board 1931-'32. Case reporter, Med. Undergrad. Society and Journal, Vice-President A.O.A.

◀ The McGill University 1933 yearbook included Drew's picture and a short paragraph about his life.

Chapter 4

Great Discoveries

After Drew graduated from McGill in 1933, he continued his research with Dr. Beattie. But when his father died in 1935, Drew returned to Washington, D.C., to be with his family. Drew continued his blood research there. He also taught at Howard University Medical School.

Columbia Medical School

In 1938, Drew received a Rockefeller Fellowship to study surgery at Columbia Medical School in New York City. He worked under John Scudder, a professor who studied blood and blood transfusions. Drew researched blood **plasma** and helped supervise a **blood bank**.

Drew (center) became a teacher at Howard University Medical School, the same school that had turned him down as a student.

Drew saw that using blood plasma could save many lives. Plasma has no red blood cells. Because red blood cells determine blood type, plasma has no blood type. A patient with any blood type can safely receive blood plasma.

Like whole blood, plasma stayed fresh for only a short time. Hospitals still faced shortages. Drew searched for a solution. He found that blood and plasma lasted longer if kept cool. But they still didn't last long enough. Finally, he developed a way to dry and store plasma for a long time. Because of Drew's research, hospitals would always have dried plasma available for patients.

Marriage

In April 1939, Drew met a college teacher named Lenore Robbins. Drew and Lenore fell in love quickly. They married in September and had their first of four children the following year.

Drew graduated from Columbia in 1940. He was the first African American ever to earn the advanced degree of Doctor of Science in Medicine.

Chapter 5

World War II

In June 1940, Drew and his family moved to Washington, D.C. Drew became an assistant professor of surgery at Howard University and a **surgeon** at Freedmen's Hospital.

Blood for Britain

Meanwhile, war raged in Europe. Germany had taken over Poland and France. Germany was bombing English cities, and Britain desperately needed blood to treat wounded soldiers.

That year, the Blood for Britain project began. Drew's former teacher Dr. Beattie was involved in the project. He contacted Drew.

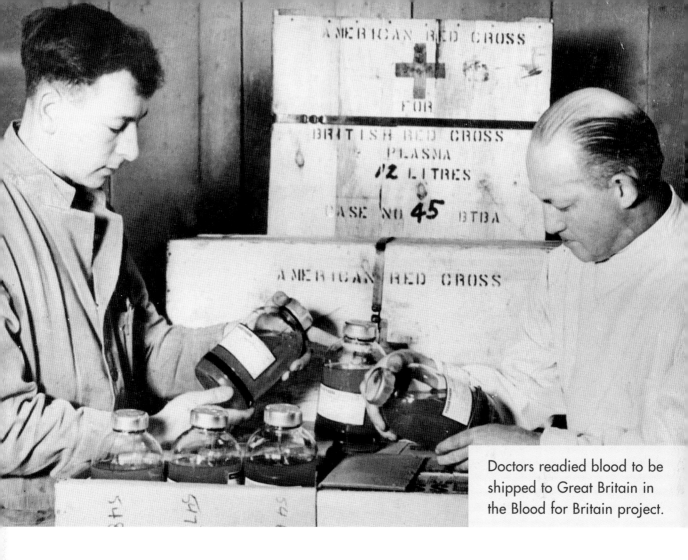

Doctors readied blood to be shipped to Great Britain in the Blood for Britain project.

Drew returned to New York. He supervised the Blood for Britain project from September 1940 through January 1941. He organized the collection and safe shipment of more than 14,500 pints (6,861 liters) of plasma.

Bloodmobiles

In February 1941, Drew became the medical director of the American Red Cross' first-ever blood collection program. The Red Cross blood bank was based in New York.

Drew needed to find as many donors as possible. Many people could not travel to the blood bank. So Drew thought of a way to bring the blood bank to the people. He started using trucks with refrigerators inside to store blood. These trucks became known as bloodmobiles. They could be used to accept donations anywhere.

Drew (left) stood with Red Cross nurses in front of the first bloodmobile.

In April 1941, Drew left the Red Cross and returned to Washington, D.C. He was accepted by the American Board of Surgery and became head of Howard University's Department of Surgery.

In November 1941, the American Red Cross announced that it would not accept blood from African Americans. Some white people didn't want to receive African American blood, even if it could save their lives.

"There is no
scientific basis
for the separation
of the bloods of
different races."
—Charles Drew

Taking a Stand

As a scientist and a
doctor, Drew knew that
the donor's race didn't
matter. Blood was blood,
no matter what the donor's
skin color was. Drew spoke
out against the policy. So
did African Americans all
over the country.

In January 1942, the Red
Cross changed its policy.
African Americans were
allowed to give blood. But
their blood had to be kept
separate. Soldiers would
only receive blood from
donors of their own race.

This news disappointed Drew. Whenever he could, he explained that the separation was unnecessary. But the Red Cross did not change the policy until 1949.

An African American man donates blood in 1944. According to Red Cross policy at that time, this man's blood would be kept separate from the blood of white donors. ▼

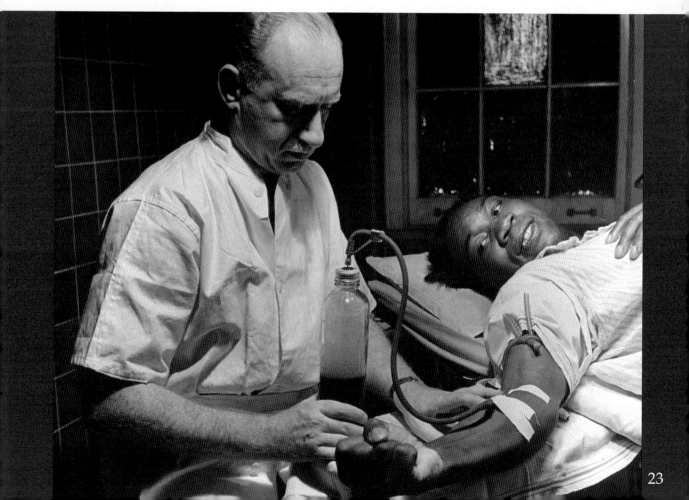

Chapter 6

Drew's Impact

Meanwhile, Drew focused on training African American doctors. At the time, black doctors had difficulty finding jobs. They were not given the same respect as white doctors. Drew hoped to change that by improving educational opportunities for black doctors. Well-trained black doctors could compete better with white doctors.

Drew's Death

On April 1, 1950, Drew was traveling with three other doctors to Tuskegee, Alabama, for a medical conference. They began driving in the middle of the night.

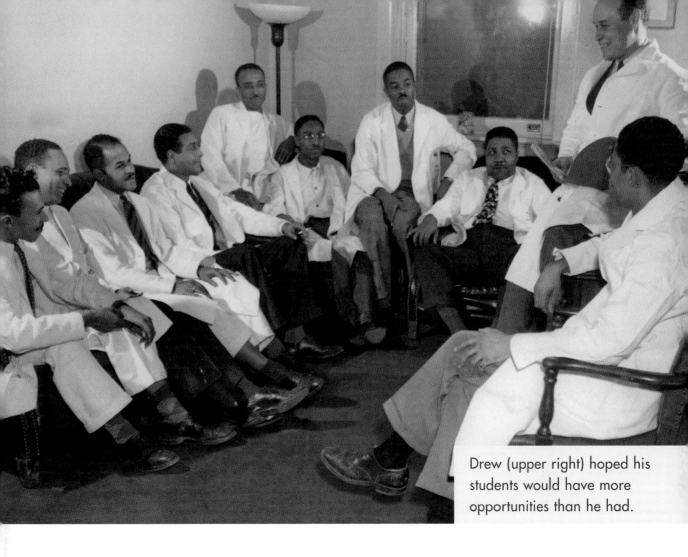

Drew (upper right) hoped his students would have more opportunities than he had.

Drew fell asleep while driving through North Carolina. The car flipped over. Drew's leg was deeply cut, and he went into shock.

▲ A postage stamp featuring Drew's portrait was released June 3, 1981.

FACT!

In 1979, the American Red Cross headquarters was renamed the Charles R. Drew Blood Center.

At the hospital, Drew received a blood transfusion. But he couldn't be saved. Drew died within two hours.

Drew's Legacy

Since his death, many groups have honored Drew. His portrait hangs in the gallery at the National Institutes of Health. He was the first African American to be included. In 1981, Drew appeared on a stamp in the U.S. Post Office's "Great Americans" series.

Drew never let his skin color decide what he could accomplish. Many people around the world owe their lives to Drew's work.

Fast Facts

Full name: Charles Richard Drew

Occupation: Physician and blood researcher

Birth: June 3, 1904

Death: April 1, 1950

Parents: Richard Thomas Drew and Nora Rosella Burrell

Siblings: 4 younger siblings

Wife: Lenore Robbins Drew

Children: Bebe, Charlene, Rhea, Charles Jr.

Hometown: Washington, D.C.

Education:
Amherst College in Massachusetts
McGill University in Quebec, Canada
Columbia University in New York

Achievements:
Developed a system of long-term storage
of blood plasma
Developed bloodmobiles
Organized national blood drives to help
soldiers during World War II

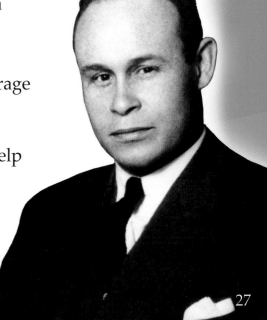

Time Line

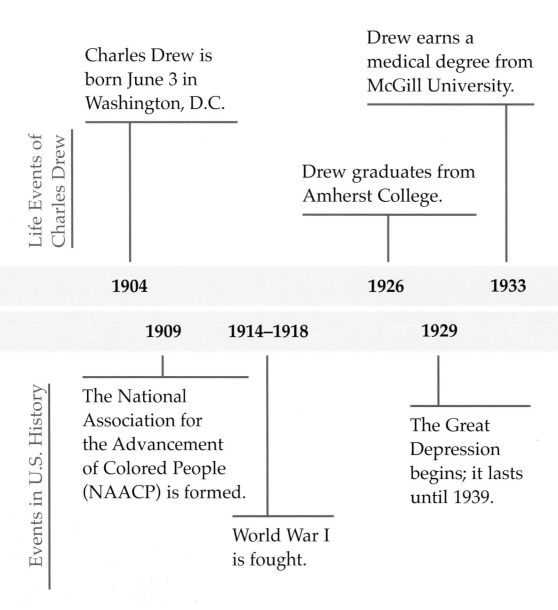

Life Events of Charles Drew

Charles Drew is born June 3 in Washington, D.C.

Drew earns a medical degree from McGill University.

Drew graduates from Amherst College.

1904 1926 1933

1909 1914–1918 1929

Events in U.S. History

The National Association for the Advancement of Colored People (NAACP) is formed.

World War I is fought.

The Great Depression begins; it lasts until 1939.

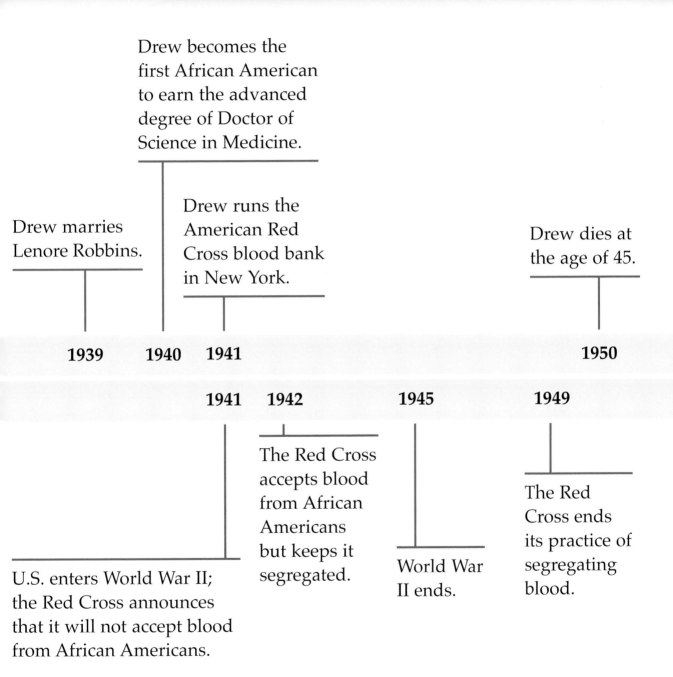

Drew becomes the first African American to earn the advanced degree of Doctor of Science in Medicine.

Drew marries Lenore Robbins.

Drew runs the American Red Cross blood bank in New York.

Drew dies at the age of 45.

1939   **1940**   **1941**   **1950**

1941   **1942**   **1945**   **1949**

The Red Cross accepts blood from African Americans but keeps it segregated.

The Red Cross ends its practice of segregating blood.

U.S. enters World War II; the Red Cross announces that it will not accept blood from African Americans.

World War II ends.

Glossary

blood bank (BLUHD BANGK)—a place where blood is donated and stored; hospitals use this stored blood to replace blood lost by someone during an operation or in an accident.

compatible (kuhm-PAT-uh-buhl)—able to be used together without difficulty

plasma (PLAZ-muh)—the clear, yellow, liquid part of blood

racism (RAY-siz-uhm)—the belief that one race is better than another race

surgeon (SUR-juhn)—a doctor who performs operations

transfusion (transs-FYOO-zhun)—the transfer of blood from one person into the body of someone else

Internet Sites

FactHound offers a safe, fun way to find Internet sites related to this book. All of the sites on FactHound have been researched by our staff.

Here's how:

1. Visit *www.facthound.com*
2. Type in this special code **0736854339** for age-appropriate sites. Or enter a search word related to this book for a more general search.
3. Click on the **Fetch It** button.

FactHound will fetch the best sites for you!

Read More

Schraff, Anne E. *Charles Drew: Pioneer in Medicine.* Famous Inventors. Berkeley Heights, N.J.: Enslow, 2003.

Schraff, Anne E. *Dr. Charles Drew: Blood Bank Innovator.* African-American Biographies. Berkeley Heights, N.J.: Enslow, 2003.

Whitehurst, Susan. *Dr. Charles Drew, Medical Pioneer.* African American Library. Chanhassen, Minn.: Child's World, 2002.

Index